written and drawn by
JOHN FARMAN

MACMILLAN
CHILDREN'S BOOKS

First published 1998 by Macmillan Children's Books
a division of Macmillan Publishers Limited
25 Eccleston Place, London SW1W 9NF
and Basingstoke

Associated companies throughout the world

ISBN 0 330 37088 X

1 3 5 7 9 8 6 4 2

A CIP catalogue record for this book is available from
the British Library.

Printed and bound in Great Britain
by Mackays of Chatham plc, Kent

☙ CONTENTS

☙ OFF WE GO!

Parents are forever telling their kids that life was much better, not only when they were young, but way back into history. ('We never had all this computer rubbish in our day, we had to amuse ourselves – just you ask your grandad.') Well, it might be true in some respects, but generally the further back you go the more dodgy life was (especially if you didn't happen to be wealthy).

The Stuart period was no exception, unless you're into plagues, fires, bloody civil wars, or never knowing, when you set out on a journey, whether highwaymen on land or pirates at sea would relieve you of your goods – or worse, your life (let alone not knowing whether you'd fall off the edge of the world).

The Stuart period began when James came to the English throne in 1603, having been King of Scotland (where he was spelt Stewart) since a baby. In this little book I hope to give you some idea of what life was like, and why, despite all the things wrong with modern life (the Spice Girls and Jeffrey Archer for instance), I'd far rather live now than then.*

By the way, any supposedly funny comments you might see at the bottom of pages in this book are by my editor, Susie. She likes to feel needed.

* Personally, I'd rather you'd lived then. Ed

Chapter 1

THE HISTORICAL BIT

Poor wee James Stuart (or Stewart) could never have been accused of having an easy early life, unless you're the sort of person who'd've liked having your mum (Mary Queen of Scots) leave you when you when you were tiny (having just blown up your dad – allegedly) and then spend most of her life in a dungeon prior to having her own head cut off on her auntie (Elizabeth)'s orders. If that wasn't bad enough, baby Jamie had to become sovereign (of Scotland), before he could even say the word.

Useless Fact No. 663

Being made sovereign as a baby ran in the family. His mother was also only one year old when crowned. Weird, eh?

In those days Scotland and England were completely separate countries with nothing but the remains of a big Roman wall (Hadrian's) between them. The English, particularly the Puritans (strict Protestants), invited James to be their king on old Queen Elizabeth's death in 1603, not because they particularly liked the idea of a Scotsman running their show, but because he was a Protestant and they were terrified of a Catholic getting the job. Elizabeth had terminated his mother, Mary, because she was involved in a Catholic plot to overthrow her (allegedly again!), and old 'Bloody' Mary who reigned before *her* had barbecued hundreds of Protestants. The Catholics and the Protestants were obviously not the best of friends, to say the least.

Pleasing the Puritans

The Puritans had become really excited about James being king, because he came from a country that prided itself on the quality of its Catholic-bashing. Unfortunately (for the Puritans) he didn't think much of their ways either and threatened to show them the door too (that's why a whole bunch of Puritans jumped into the *Mayflower* in 1620, and pushed off to find North America, Disneyland and all that).

Pleasing the Catholics

The Catholics also got a bit excited when James became king, because Mary Queen of Scots, his mum, was a Catholic (albeit a dead Catholic), and it followed that life might be just a little kinder to them. No such luck. They were forgetting that many of the super-rich politicians (whose families had been given whopping great shares of the lands that had been nicked by naughty old Henry VIII when he blitzed all the Catholic monasteries) would do practically anything to prevent their return.*

Guy Fawkes

All this provided the setting for the famous Gunpowder Plot, in which that poor guy (Guy) was caught red-handed, in the cellars of the Houses of Parliament, sitting on 36 barrels of gunpowder, with a lighted taper in his hand (a trifle suspicious, what!). He and his Catholic mates had wanted to take out the sovereign and all his politicians in one big bang – which has a certain appeal, don't you think? This was to act as the starting pistol for a massive Catholic uprising throughout the land.

OKAY, I ADMIT IT DOES LOOK A LITTLE SUSPICIOUS

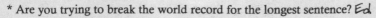

* Are you trying to break the world record for the longest sentence? Ed

Useless Fact No. 666

Just to show how cross the authorities were with him, Guy Fawkes and his mates were tortured to the point of severe eye-watering, and then hung, drawn and quartered in a most uncomfortable manner.

Didn't James Do Well?

Despite being a bit of a show-off and running an extravagant and extremely 'gay' court, James I managed to do quite well in his reign. He ended the long war with Spain (for about ten minutes) and managed against all odds to keep the Catholics and the Puritans apart.

Things started to go wrong because he believed that he had a God-given right to do just about anything he pleased without bothering to ask the government . . . All very well, but by the time he died, his government owed over £1 million (an absolute fortune in those days) and – oh yes – he'd somehow got us into another war with Spain.

Useless Fact No. 669

James I was pretty much ahead of his time when he blathered on and on about smoking. Not because it was bad for you but because it made men's 'sweet breath smell'. Oh yeh!

Here Comes Charlie

Charles I, James's son, was a bit weedy by all accounts – small, stammering, shifty and completely unreliable (sounds like my editor*). He proved the latter, later, by going out and marrying Henrietta, the King of Spain's daughter. Good news in one way (hands across the sea, friends and neighbours, and all that) but terrible when you consider her religion, which was – yup, you've got it – Catholic!

With the help of his ex-dad's ex-boyfriend, the Earl of Buckingham, Charles then managed to slip us neatly into a war with Spain and France – both together this time.

Now, wars tend to cost money and Charles didn't have any. Parliament, who by this time hated both Charles and Buckingham, not only refused to help but gave the big thumbs-down to any rise in taxes to pay for them. When his mate Buckingham was assassinated in 1628, Charles thought, 'Blow this, I can rule perfectly well without any rotten old parliament.' And he did.

How to make yourself unpopular in five easy moves

1. Having made himself very much *not* flavour of the month with the ruling classes, he then decided to do the same with his less-loyal-by-the-minute poorer subjects by ordering them to feed all his soldiers – for free – and on demand.
2. Still short of cash, he then hit the rich landowners and taxed them to within an inch of their lives. This, as you might imagine, was not really to their liking.
3. Then, still short of the old readies, he thought he'd tax all those that lived near the sea (the Ship Tax).
4. Finally, having not offended quite enough people, he went

* You're fired. Ed

and told the Scots who they should worship, which hacked them off so much they decided to invade.

5. By now, Parliament had had it up to here with Charles and refused to sanction the looming war. Undaunted, Charles gathered together the remnants of his army and tried to arrest Parliament – but they all ran away.

There was only one thing for it: Civil War. The King and the Catholics (the Cavaliers or Royalists) were on one side and Parliament and the Puritans (the Roundheads or Parliamentarians) led by Oliver Cromwell, on the other.

Useless Fact No. 671

The Roundheads were the Roundheads because their heads were round (owing to very short haircuts). The Cavaliers were called the Cavaliers because theirs weren't. (Actually, it was because they were horsemen or dressed like horsemen.)

Useless Fact No. 672

The Roundheads did a really smart deal with the Scots, promising that England would become Presbyterian (McChristians) if they joined their side.

To cut a very, very, long and extremely bloody story very, very short, the Roundheads won,* but then a scrap broke out between Cromwell's superbly trained army of bullyboys (the New Model Army) and an odd cocktail of the Scots, the English Presbyterians and what was left of the Royalists. It all ended with poor old Charles having his dear little head ceremoniously removed from his dear little shoulders. He was the first and last (so far) English monarch to be executed. Was that the end of the Stuarts? Read on.

* Well done. You've dismissed one of the most significant periods of our history in one sentence. Ed
I'm in a hurry – anyway, I'm going to do a whole other book about it. JF

Anyone for King?

Oliver Cromwell didn't want to be the king (would you, after what happened to Charles?) and nor did anyone else really want him to either, so for eleven years England was kingless with Ollie in charge. In his official role as Lord Protector of the Commonwealth of England, which I think sounds far flasher than just plain 'King', he divided the country into eleven districts – each with a troop of soldiers, to make sure there wouldn't be another Royalist uprising.

Useless Fact No. 677

Life under the Puritan Cromwell was no laughing matter. He banned pubs, theatres, cock-fighting, bear-baiting, horse-racing and anything else that had helped to make England 'Merrie'. On Sundays working, or playing games, or eating or even walking (except to church) were forbidden – on pain of death. As for smiling – forget it!

Charles II

Cromwell died in 1658 and his lad, Richard, got the top job. But he was pretty useless and almost immediately the much-relieved English invited Charles I's son, Charles II, back from exile. In the meantime, wee Charlie had been being King of the Scots. (Are you following all this?) All's well that ends well, I expect he thought.

Useless Fact No. 679

To say the English were pleased to see Charles was a bit of an understatement. All along the route the walls were hung with fine silks and embroideries, every church-bell pealed and all the fountains in London spurted red wine. I bet the meanies wouldn't do that nowadays!

But this Charles was nothing like his old man, being awfully ugly, lazy and flippant, and fond of chasing all the pretty girls around the court, despite being married to the deeply prim and proper Catherine of Braganza. Charles was understandably rather cross with all Cromwell's chums that had helped get his father executed and managed to execute them back. He then dug up the somewhat smelly Cromwell, who'd annoyingly died of natural causes (a rare feat in those days), and had his head cut off too – which he stuck on a pike at Westminster.

VERY FUNNY MR FARMAN

Useless Fact No. 681

One of Charles II's countless girlfriends was the famous actress and orange salesperson, Nell Gwyn. Talking of girlfriends, he fathered countless royal b . . . er, illegitimate children.

Foreign Troubles

OK, Charles was lazy, but he was in no way daft, and he was determined to see out his reign despite other ideas from abroad. Catholic France, as usual, was causing probs. It was by far the most powerful country in Europe and meant to show everyone, especially the English and Dutch, just who was *le boss*. Just to complicate matters, Charles managed to get involved in a war against the Dutch (this all sounds like the European Cup) and the Dutch fleet even sailed up the Medway and destroyed our nice navy in Chatham before the Treaty of Breda was signed in 1667.

Health Alert!

But England had more to worry about than a few Dutch boats. In 1665 the bubonic plague (or Black Death) broke out which was to kill 68,595* in London alone, and a year later the Great Fire raged through London leaving 200,000 people homeless (see Chapter 8).

Who Next?

Charles and Catherine had no proper (legitimate) children despite all the others that he'd fathered and she hadn't mothered. This became a bit of a poser as it was obvious that when Charles II died, the next in line would be none other than his younger brother James who was . . . Catholic.

* My book says it was 68,596. Ed
What's one plague victim between friends? JF

Between 1679 and 1681 it looked as if England was going to pull itself apart again in another civil war between all those who liked James (called Tories) and all those who didn't (called Whigs). Charles cleverly avoided war by overruling Parliament, and by the time he went to the great throne in the sky in 1685, the Tories had the upper hand and, throne-wise, the Stuarts had never been safer.

James II

Poor old England had finally come round to thinking that James might be right for the throne. Tough luck! He wasn't. Gruesome rumours soon floated across the Channel about French Protestants being tortured and killed and the English quickly became paranoid that their Catholic James might get ideas.

James, a reasonably pleasant sort of bloke (for a king), couldn't work out why the Catholics were so unpopular in England, and tried to make their life a bit easier by allowing them to worship when and where they wanted. He also promised that the Anglicans could continue the Anglican church – which was rather nice of him (considering he was a Catholic). But he didn't like those Puritans one bit and continued to hunt them down. To help teach them a lesson he appointed a judge called Jeffreys, who he'd admired ever since Jeffreys had tried the admittedly rather rotten rebel Titus Oates and had him lashed 3,000 times all the way across London.

Monmouth's Rebellion

This horrid treatment of the Puritans caused a bunch of Whigs, who'd been forced to live in Holland, to plan a rebellion, which was timed to go with off with one in Scotland. Their leader, the Duke of Monmouth, the illegitimate son of Charles II and chief contender for the throne, landed in Dorset and formed a rather pathetic little army of Protestants determined to give the Catholics and the Anglicans a lesson they'd never forget.

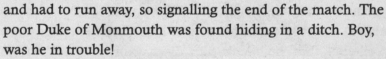

Useless Fact No. 683
Monmouth's army's equipment left a lot to be desired. Rusty old swords, decrepit muskets and poles with scythes tied to the ends to make them look like pikes.*

The rebel army attacked the King's army while they were asleep in Somerset, but ran out of ammo before dawn and had to run away, so signalling the end of the match. The poor Duke of Monmouth was found hiding in a ditch. Boy, was he in trouble!

The Cruellest Cut
Monmouth's death was well worth reporting. Before the well-known executioner Jack Ketch was appointed to do the deadly deed, the Duke had been a right sissy – weeping and begging on his knees to be spared for simply ages.

Ketch was famous, not because he was so brilliant at the old head removal, but because he wasn't. This time was to be no

* Oh no, not the pike joke again. Ed

exception. Having chopped at poor Monmouth's neck three times without managing to cut right through, he flung down his axe in a right temper and said he wasn't playing any more. It was only after officials threatened him with a similar fate that he administered two more blows, but he still failed to remove the head completely.

Meanwhile, presumably, the Duke, with typical aristocratic stiff upper lip (and neck), had been waiting patiently. In the end Mr Ketch had to finish off the grizzly job with his knife. Ow.

Judge Jeffreys

Now there's judges and judges, but by far the cruellest in England's history was the aforementioned George Jeffreys, a real sweetheart who was in charge of trying all the Puritan supporters of the Duke of Monmouth. He really didn't muck about, deporting 800 to slavery in the West Indies and leaving another 300 dangling by the roadsides like Christmas decorations (or Christian decorations?), as a warning to all those who might have been thinking along the same lines.

Child Alert!

All this really got up the noses of the Protestant lords, who went into furious overdrive when, after two daughters, Mary and Anne, James II and his wife had a boy-child (oh my lord – not another Catholic heir to the throne).

Civil war loomed again with armies and remnants of armies (James had disbanded his) just dying (literally) to get at each other. By the beginning of 1668 everyone was at each other's throats. On June 30, after much consultation, the Protestants sent a rather sneaky letter to William of Orange (James II's nephew) and his wife Mary (James II's daughter*), who were the Protestant rulers of Holland, asking if they'd care to come over and rule us too. Bit of a cheek when you think about it.

When the Oranges landed in 1688, soldiers flocked to join their side, which sort of annoyed James, especially as Dutch Will was his son-in-law and especially as half of the flocking soldiers were from his own army. However, James thought about it for five minutes and, no doubt saying 'blow this for a game of soldiers', promptly bought a one-way ticket to France, never to be seen in England again.

Useless Fact No. 685

When news of the invasion arrived, an extremely anxious able-seaman Jeffreys tried to enlist on the next boat out of England but was recognized and promptly sent to the Bloody Tower, where he died.

---

* No wonder they were all a bit mad. Ed

Son and Grandson

In exile, James's son and grandson became the Old Pretender (James Edward Stuart) and Young Pretender (Charles Edward Stuart, or Bonnie Prince Charlie), and they both (separately) came back to these shores to annoy us lots and try to claim the throne. They finally gave up in 1715 and 1746 (respectively).

Chapter 2

THE RESTORATION OF KING AND CULTURE

Before Cromwell and his beastly Puritans knocked the entertainment business for six, the theatre was a booming industry – thanks to one bloke in particular. The 'Bard of Avon', William Shakespeare, was probably England's most popular and prolific playwright.

Useless Fact No. 688

James I, unfortunately, wasn't that impressed, describing our Will's masterpiece *Macbeth* as 'the most weak, ridiculous play that I ever saw in my life'. I wonder what he'd have made of stuff like *Starlight Express*?

EVER CONSIDERED MUSICALS MR SHAKESPEARE?

Play Time

There were six theatres in London at the time, including the Globe – of which there's a perfect (if a bit sanitized) modern-day replica in London. Theatres were pretty wacky in those days: the audience could and did walk about, shout insults, throw things (I wish!) and eat, drink and generally be merrie during performances.

There were also masques, which were little more than hugely opulent fashion statements, much loved by James I and his wife, and put on by rich amateurs from the Court. In a way they took over from the theatres which were already losing ground when the Puritans, who condemned everything, closed them for immorality and prosecuted the actors as rogues.

Useless Fact No. 691

Double-standard time. Head Puritan, Ollie Cromwell, was known to be a closet music fan and gave permission for the very first English opera, *The Siege of Rhodes*, in 1656.

Names to drop from James I's time

John Donne
Poet and preacher

Francis Bacon
Philosopher

Samuel Pepys
Man who kept a diary

Er . . .*

* Get on with it. Ed

About Turn

The reign of Charles II is quite famous in the history of our art. It was an age known as the Restoration, a term used to celebrate having a king back again. But it was much more than that, as it also referred to the fun period following that awful era of puerile Puritanism, when everything that people thought was good and enjoyable turned out to be bad for them. It was like taking the cover off a canary cage. Suddenly England could shake itself down and sing again.*

The Theatre Royal, Drury Lane (still there), opened in 1674, featuring female actors for the first time. It especially attracted the restored King Charles II (always out for a good time) who was known to be a bit of an old lech.

Useless Fact No. 693

Nell Gwyn, one of Charles' many mistresses, was one of the first women to perform on the London stage. But the audiences were still terribly behaved…

'One half of the play they spend in noise and brawl,
Sleep out the rest, then wake and damn it all.'

After the exile of Charles' brother James, there followed two rather prim Stuart Queens (James's sisters, Mary and Anne) who really weren't into the rudeness of it all, turning their noses up at all the bloody dramas and smutty comedies that had come along after the Restoration.

Poetry and Proper Books

There were a lot of good poems written in Puritan times by men like Ben Jonson and, oddly enough, the staunch Puritan John Milton. Other writers like Jonathan Swift (of *Gulliver's*

* What!? Ed

Travels fame) wrote political pieces in the news-sheets, taking the mickey out of any party that they didn't care for.

Architecture

Before the Great Fire there had been a famous architect called Inigo Jones (sounds more like a cowboy to me), the hugely gifted son of a clothworker, who'd visited Italy and had been knocked sideways by the work of the Paduan architect, Palladio (loads of columns and sloping roofs and things*). This, he determined, would fill the gap when the Tudor Gothic style that had been all the rage back home passed its sell-by date. He became the King's advisor on all things building-wise, a task which he carried out with *molto* style and *mucho* panache.

Useless Fact No. 696
You can still see the beautiful St Paul's Church in Covent Garden, designed by Mr Jones and finished in 1633.

After the Fire

Disasters can be quite good for cities, because they usually mean you can start again, avoiding all the blunders that went before. Post-fire London was no exception. With four-fifths of the city in smouldering ashes, there had to be a rebuilding plan pretty darn quick. A chap named Christopher Wren, a prominent scientist and all-round clever-clogs, who was also a great fan of Italian buildings, came up with an elaborate plan. Sadly, the government didn't go for his scheme because the merchants and shopkeepers couldn't wait to put up their 'open' signs again, and so voted for something simpler. But Wren did get to design and build lots of churches (God is far more

* How very concisely and brilliantly put. Ed

patient), many of which are still standing (including the fabulous St Paul's Cathedral). It has been said that if Christopher Wren had had his way, London would have rivalled Florence or Venice (instead of Slough) in beauty.

Useless Fact No. 697

Sir Christopher Wren's amazing plans were submitted only a few days after the fire . . . Very suspicious – it would have made me wonder if he'd started the fire in the first place!

THAT'LL DO NICELY

Purcell Rules

Even if they're not into classical music, most people will admit that composer Henry Purcell (1659–1695) was probably the greatest and most versatile musician that England ever produced (apart from Des O'Connor, of course). Our Henry was a bit a child prodigy by all accounts (probably got Grade 8 piano at six months) and became the organist at Westminster Abbey when still a young lad (20). Not content with simply playing with his organ all day, he wrote music for piano, orchestra and even an opera – *Dido and Aeneas*. His beautifully simple, haunting melodies and magnificently stirring pieces for full orchestra blew away the post-Puritan gloom for ever and established an interest in fine music among the British people which has lasted to this day.*

* And that, I hope, is the end of today's lecture. Ed

☁ Chapter 3

☁ WHAT TO EAT?

Unlike these days when you can get practically any sort of food, anywhere, at any time of year, in Stuart times the food eaten in the average farmhouse – and indeed the posh houses – had to be seasonal.

Lent Rules

Everyone took Lent really seriously and ate only fish (as you were supposed to) – fresh, if they lived near a river or the sea, and salted if not. Meat was not eaten, partly for religious reasons, partly due to ancient customs, partly to be nice to the fishermen, but mostly, if truth be told, because there wasn't any (except salted) at that time of year. All the cows, sheep and pigs were sentenced to death at the midsummer feast and were eaten throughout the winter. Having said that, you'd've practically tripped over the rabbits, hares and other game in the fields of Olde England.

Xmas Cheer

At Christmas, during the twelve days when there really wasn't any point working on the land, rich and not quite so rich alike gorged themselves silly on brawn (jellied meat from a pig's head – yum yum!), fowl, chickens, turkeys, mince pies and plum pudding and a huge joint of beef stuck with sprigs of rosemary.

After Christmas the poor had a habit of nearly starving, and were only saved by a diet of cheese and rough bread.

Poor People's Food

Vegetables weren't grown much (only in people's backyards), purely because they weren't regarded as a commercial crop. To be honest, peasant folk didn't see the point of vegetables and really didn't eat their greens like they should have (cabbage was labelled 'windy meat').

As for the humble spud, it was either unheard of or despised – until years later when it was all some poor beggars had to eat. It was a similar story with fruit, apart from apples, which were grown in orchards for cider making. If you won't eat 'em, drink 'em.

Your average, up-at-dawn farm worker would have his breakfast around 6.30 – usually bread and beer. (It's worth noting that the beer we drink these days would have the average serf flat on his back, as their stuff was as weak as gnats' pee. As beer was the staple drink of the poor, it was often warmed, spiced or sweetened to appeal to women and children – imagine that these days.) Most of the milk that they could squeeze out of their cows went into butter and cheese making, with any left-overs for babies and invalids.

Useless Fact No. 699
Spirits were unheard of for ordinary people until the great gin epidemic of the eighteenth century. Tea and coffee were only really known in trendy London and were hideously expensive.

A farm worker would have lunch at midday and supper at six in the evening. If his boss gave him his meals, his wages would be cut accordingly (there was no such thing as a free lunch – even in Stuart times!). Don't feel too sorry for him, though – just remember Daniel Defoe's famous comment: *'Compared with other countries the English common people fed magnificently.'* I wonder what yer average farmworker would have said about that.

Enclosure Blues
The fencing-off of the land by its owners for the more intensive growing of crops (rather than the grazing of tenants' sheep)*

* Are crops more likely to escape than sheep? Ed

was a near disaster. The enclosures really annoyed the poor serfs and cottagers. England's green and pleasant land had, since time began, belonged to everybody to graze their beasts, collect wood and hay and run about on. In fact, without this freedom of the land, the peasants were going to find it very difficult to survive. But nobody cared what the peasants thought, anyway. Let's move on to something a bit jollier.

Chapter 4

HAVING FUN –
STUART STYLE

England was a great place if you liked forests and murdering all the sweet little cuddly creatures that lived in 'em. Just about everyone in the countryside (which was just about everyone) would hunt down the enormous herds of deer, wild pigs and rabbits (herds of rabbits?) which provided, at certain times of the year, a substantial proportion of the English people's meat intake. It was not unknown for whole villages to take to the woods with clubs, nets and savage dogs to massacre anything of a non-vegetable nature that moved.

PSST–THEY'RE COMING

Peasant Poaching

This was OK if the forest was on common land. It was different if it was on the Lord of the Manor's estate. In earlier days the poor were allowed a small share of the hunt spoils (fox pie?) or even to snare rabbits and catch fish on their own. Then the meanie parliament passed an act forbidding such practices and creating the new crime of 'poaching'. After that, hunting became the major hobby of the well-to-do and a life-or-death undercover operation for the poor. In fact, some rich landowners thought their only function in life was to hunt during the day, and sing rude songs in alehouses in the evenings, before going home drunk to dine with the ladies of the house – sounds fine to me!

Useless Fact No. 701

The lord of the manor was usually the local MP and magistrate as well, so his other great sport was trying and punishing the poor peasant poacher. Even better, 'court sessions' would be held in the comfort of the boss's own home.

In those days, before political correctness and the endangered species act, otters were speared, badgers were dug up and torn to shreds, and foxes were chased by hounds – not necessarily because they were vermin but because it was thought to be fun. Sick or what? Oddly enough, the shooting of animals and game birds (partridge and pheasant) with guns was forbidden, so they used nets and pet hawks.

Useless Fact No. 703

The colourful but somewhat stupid peasant* that we know and love today was introduced by the Romans from the east to adorn their villas. The poor things have been hiding in the deepest forests ever since they left.

* Shouldn't that read 'pheasant'? Ed

And the Ladies . . .

While the men were away from home hunting, the women had to confine themselves to their household duties. These included brewing the beer, salting the meat, preserving the fruit, sewing, organizing the daily cooking and, usually, having the babies. In areas where there were few doctors they often became absorbed in the art of healing, although many thought that the use of charms, potions and white magic seemed much more like witchcraft than anything else.

Country Games

The village green was the centre for the humbler folk's fun in Stuart times. In the summer, boys and girls skipped round the maypole in a rather soppy manner, while the old 'uns played skittles, bowls, or a primitive version of cricket.

Footie Scrum

Football was played too, but it was more or less a glorified punch-up (so what's changed?), much closer to rugby than the football we know now. Best of all, if you lived out in the sticks, were the regular fairs which were visited by pedlars, musicians and other touring entertainers.

Town Fun

It has to be said that the Stuart townies were a dead cruel bunch when it came to play-time. They liked nothing better than watching a large wild beast being torn to shreds by mastiffs (big snarly dogs) driven mad by hunger. Favourite of all were huge black bears, imported from northern Europe, blinded, chained to poles and goaded till jolly cross. Often these bears would rip the dogs apart to the delight of the crowd and toss bits of them into the audience. Sometimes the men who ran the baiting rings managed to get hold of the odd lion or tiger and would set the dogs on them too. Even monkeys were trained to join in the fun. Very nasty and not funny.

I SAY_ WOULD YOU CARE TO GO FIRST ?

Cock-fighting was the most popular; fortunes were won or lost on the poor cluckers that were fitted with vicious spurs to inflict the maximum damage on each other. The loser, by the way, always ended up dead. Right back from Elizabethan days, nobility and royalty were hooked on these severely disgusting 'sports'.

Gentler Pursuits

Following the introduction of coffee in 1652, strange new institutions called Coffee (and Chocolate) Houses sprang up. It seems difficult to imagine that anything as ordinary as a non-alcoholic hot drink (and an expensive one at that) could have created such a craze, but soon there were some 500 coffee houses in London. They became the meeting places for all men of business and some of the great institutions like Lloyds of London and the Stock Exchange grew out of them.

With no telly or radio people went to bed much earlier in those days. Reading? Books were still really expensive and, let's face it, candlelight gets pretty tiring on the old eyes after an hour or two. Games? Cards was the big craze at the time, and played by men and women alike. Dancing? Yes, people loved dancing, either formally at sniffy private parties, or in the hundreds of taverns, which were always raucous and very rough. Bit like my local on a Friday night.

* Hens cluck. Cocks crow. Ed
Editors nag. JF

Chapter 5

A WOMAN'S LOT

Girls were hardly educated at all, as it was regarded as a waste of time, but they weren't allowed to sit around and twiddle their thumbs either. On top of all the boring housework, it was OK for upper-class girls to make tapestries, write rather yucky, somewhat soppy poetry or learn music to entertain the menfolk when they came home plastered.

Getting Hitched

The poor dears were usually married off at between the ages of thirteen and eighteen (their husbands would be between fifteen and twenty-eight). Even then there wasn't much fun for the ladies, as the chaps usually went straight off after the wedding with their tutors to Europe for a couple of years, or to university to finish their 'education'.

Marriages were 'arranged' among the upper classes, which must have been gut-wrenchingly embarrassing. After the parents had completed the negotiations, the young man would be expected to visit the poor girl to make his formal advances with not so much as a quick snog behind the bike sheds before the big day. The only upside to this barbarous practice was that just about everyone got someone – even the ones with bad breath. The odd thing is that many of these manufactured relationships turned into real affection. Just goes to show that loads of choice isn't always a good thing, I suppose.

Lower down in the social orders, the matches made were not so much to do with whether the girl was of a good (for 'good', read 'rich') family, but whether she'd be a strong worker and physically robust enough to drop a fair number of nippers to help on the farm. Children were regarded almost as a commercial asset amongst the poor. Quite right too – all children should be earning their keep by age six at the latest.*

* You sure know how to charm your readers, don't you? Ed

Chapter 6

THE CURSE OF RELIGION

To heathens like me, the difference between all the many religions is a bit of a mystery – God's just God in my book. But in Stuart England, religion was all the rage and it had a stranglehold on every aspect of domestic and political life. For starters, everyone was expected to go to church three times on Sunday, and the church controlled all the schools and universities. Unlike these days, when you can enjoy a different religion every day of the year (should you be barmy enough) there were only three main denominations: the Anglicans, the Puritans and the Catholics.

The Anglicans
Up till the early sixteenth century all Europe had been Catholic. But in 1534 Henry VIII, as a dead obvious ruse to part-exchange his old wife for a new one, had made himself head of the English Protestant Church but kept on a few Catholic features like the special outfits they wore and various old terms like 'bishop'; this was called the Reformation and was when the Christians decided to go two different ways.

The Puritans
But that wasn't enough for the hardliners who wanted any trace of the hated Catholicism removed. These extremists were

called Puritans and were to be seriously avoided (unless you hate fun or Christmas).

WHAT'S THIS I HEAR ABOUT YOU LAUGHING?

When Charles II came back in 1660, after Cromwell's miserable years as the Lord Protector, the Puritans were given an especially hard time; their clergymen being sacked from the Church of England, and the rest being prevented from having any decent jobs, which upset them no end.*

Anything Goes . . . Almost!

In 1689, new Protestant rulers William III and Mary II passed a very polite Toleration Act, which basically allowed everyone to pray as they wished, but the English Protestants still kept their fingers crossed where Roman Catholics were concerned.

The Catholics

Say 'Catholic' to an Englishman in the seventeenth century and he'd say 'enemy'. They just wouldn't have them in the house. It all harked back to the constant wars with the Catholic French and Spanish . . . No red-blooded Englishman was

* I thought you said that being miserable made them happy. Ed

prepared to forget the way the cheeky Armada tried to invade our shores.

Relations weren't improved when they tried to blow up Parliament in 1605 or when Charles I went and married one of 'em. The English were to remain scared of all Catholics throughout the Stuart era and this fear eventually got Catholic King James II fired when he tried to improve their lot.

Useless Fact No. 704

Things eventually sorted themselves out in England over the following centuries, but the troubles in Ireland between the 'Proddies' and the Catholics go on to this day – though few can remember what the original argument was about. Blame the Stuarts, I say!

All jolly complicated, so here's a quick run-down, religion-wise, of the Stuarts:

1605:   Catholic Guy Fawkes tries to blow up Protestant King James I and Parliament.

1611:   Protestant King James I authorizes the Authorized Version of the Bible, to replace the various different versions that were being used.

1625:   Charles I comes to the throne. Not Catholic but pretty High Church.

1642:   Civil War breaks out between Puritan Protestant Cromwell and sort-of-Catholic Charles I.

1648–59: Eleven years of Puritan rule. The Lord Protector, Oliver Cromwell, in charge. No fun. No parties.

1660:   Charles II. Protestant but with Catholic leanings and a Catholic wife. On his deathbed he confessed to being a Roman Catholic.

1685:   James II. Full-blown Roman Catholic.

1689:   William and Mary, by request of the people. Protestant!

1702:   Anne, Mary's sister. Protestant again!

So there!

In 1701 the Act of Settlement was passed, which said that all future monarchs must be members of the Church of England. This made the Protestants jolly relieved, and annoyed the Catholics no end, dashing the hopes of the Old and Young Pretenders, still in exile in France.

Chapter 7

A BIT ABOUT THE COUNTRY AND A LOT ABOUT THE TOWN

At this time, 80% of the English were farmers and had a sensible habit of living near their crops and animals in small hamlets and villages. Physically, England was slowly changing. Having been mostly wild heath or marshland broken up by the remnants of the massive forests, the great expanses were gradually being enclosed by walls and hedgerows, a process that went on right into the 1800s, as more and more people tried to grab bits of land for themselves. The rest of the population lived in the small cities and towns that were all pretty weeny compared to the overcrowded, polluted monsters that we have to endure today. Even the three biggest (except for London) – Bristol, Norwich and York – only had 20,000 people apiece.

Really Useless Fact No. 707
The 1991 population figures for those three cities are:
York: 100,000
Bristol: 400,000
Norwich: 120,000

These days, if a celebrity breaks wind in Manchester the news will be reported to the rest of Britain within a couple of hours. Those days, communications were practically non-existent and letters took ages to arrive. This meant that the towns had far less influence over the country than they do these days, even though the townspeople believed they were superior (no change there then).

Town Time

Most of the bigger towns were given charters (a piece of paper saying you could do something) by the King (provided they were nice to him) which meant they could select their own mayors, aldermen and councillors. (It was probably just that the King couldn't be bothered.) Most towns were surrounded by high protective walls with massive shuttable gates,* which were a hangover from medieval days. When there were plagues about these became particularly useful in keeping out infectious refugees.

Pick and Choose

The townspeople were not only picky about germ-carrying strangers, they were also very selective when it came to letting in other kinds of riff-raff. Wastrels and untrained vagabonds were sent back along the road from whence they came, while those that *did* work within the walls were given good apprenticeship training in their various trades.

However, merchants and shopkeepers weren't allowed to take kids from anything less than yeoman (small landowners) stock, which again made it practically impossible for the country poor to improve their lot.

In the towns every trade or craft was done at home, as no factories, as we know them, existed. Employers and workers would usually work side by side in the cramped conditions of the boss's house.

Building for the Future

It is amazing how many times a house has to be burned down before the owner realizes that building it out of wood and straw might not be the smartest idea in the world. The Stuarts finally got the message and, just like those Three Little Piggies, began to use stone and bricks. Admittedly, the well-to-do were the first to catch on with the new and expensive building techniques, but that was nothing new.

* Aren't all gates shuttable? Ed

Building Pretty

One often wonders why all the houses and farm buildings built in those days look so much prettier than the artificial-looking junk we throw up these days.*

The reasons are quite simple . . .

 There were more wood and stone supplies than you could possibly cut down or dig up.

There was masses of cheap man-power to do it.

Builders took far longer to do things and had a real pride in their craftsmanship. (That really does sound like a long time ago.)

Most of all, however, unlike the nasty modern stuff used these days, natural materials were taken from the same area where the houses were to sit and therefore they didn't stand out like sore thumbs.

* You're beginning to sound like Prince Charles! Ed

The Rich

If wealthy people built great houses in Tudor times, the Stuarts went even further, probably because they were even richer. The town houses were large and imposing, with servants' quarters, kitchen, gardens, stables and coach-houses.

But the real biggies were built in the country by a new nobility which had started in Tudor times and which was added to by Charles II.

Useless Fact No. 709

Charles II actually sold off titles like Duke or Baron (prices started at around ten grand) to anyone who could stump up the cash to pay off his debts.

Many of the fabulous mansions and stately homes, with their high vaulted dining halls, magnificent tapestries, suits of armour, etc. – that the likes of you or I have to pay to visit (unless you're a lord or a lady*) – were built in these times.

The Not Quite So Rich

Below the nobility there was a new breed of nouveau-riche merchants, foreign traders and lawyers, all anxious to have large stately piles (if you'll pardon the expression) to fool others into thinking they were out of the very top drawer (which, of course, never works).

Useless Fact No. 712

These days just one article of Stuart furniture, like an old sideboard, from one of these places, could be worth more than your average two-up, two-down house. Just you watch one of those boring antiques shows if you don't believe me.

* Very likely. Ed

The Average

Lower down the social ladder, successful tradesmen or farmers lived in houses that we'd still regard as rather posh, with several bedrooms, reception rooms, servants' quarters and set in acres of land.

The Poor

The average poorer farmer would live in a small but well-built thatched cottage; while the labourer and his family would have to make do with the primitive wattle and daub hut (mud on woven sticks) that he and his like had put up with for centuries. These seldom had a chimney, or windows (glass was really pricey) and were usually full to bursting point with aunties, grannies, kiddies and pets, etc.

Shortly before the Stuart era began, an Act was passed forbidding more than one family from living in any one cottage. Although a bit of a cheek, this must have been a Godsend if you were unlucky enough to have both sets of in-laws knocking on your door.

The Very Poor

Up to this time, poor families usually slept on rough straw pallets but, by the end of the seventeenth century, many had collapsible trundle beds with proper flock or feather mattresses. As for sanitary arrangements, it was either 'bucket and chuck it' or out the back and behind the hedge, come rain or shine – like it or lump it!

Chapter 8

PLAGUES AND FIRES AND SPOTS
(It Never Rains But It Pours)

When Charles II arrived, newly restored to his father's throne, the fountains, which were all over London and supplied all its water, flowed with red wine, which sounds rather splendid if you ask me.* Water would normally have been taken straight from the Thames. Not a wise move, as you can no doubt imagine what was tipped into the river from a city with no proper rubbish disposal system and worse – no sewers. With hardly any reservoirs to collect rainwater, it was often in short supply, so hardly anyone, rich or poor, ever washed their clothes, their hair (or their wigs) or their bodies, which all provided perfect mobile homes for lice and fleas.

Useless Fact No. 715
A neat way of avoiding the old smelly bod prob was to smother oneself from head to foot in oils and perfumes and carry a nosegay (bunch, to you) of flowers to avoid catching a whiff of anyone else.

* You've already said this. Ed
I know – I like it. JF

I SAY CHARLES — DASHED FINE PERFUME YOU'RE WEARING

Fleas on the Move

Now fleas have never been too fussy about where they live, so when a bunch of dirty rats arrived by boat from the Far East, their passengers (Arab fleas) quite fancied a change of address and quickly jumped on to the unsuspecting Londoners. It was these grubby little tourists that carried the deadly plague (while feeling perfectly OK themselves) which hit in 1665.*

Here We Go

Bubonic plague was first observed at the start of the summer of 1665 in the mega-poor area of St Giles which was already struggling with a bout of smallpox. The poverty-stricken natives barely survived in the teeming and disgusting tenements that had always been an epidemic waiting to happen. A Dr Nathaniel Hodges was called to see a young man with two angry swellings (later known as plague tokens),

* That's exactly 300 years before my birthday. Ed
That makes two huge disasters in 300 years! JF

one on each thigh. Surprisingly, the young chap recovered, but those that followed weren't so lucky. .

At first it was thought that dogs and cats were the carriers, and special pet murderers (the opposite of Animal Rescue) were employed to seek out and destroy any they came across at a penny a time.

Search Me!

In the early days of the plague, women were paid to check all dead bodies for the cause of death – a rotten job, but someone had to do it. These 'searchers' were given tuppence for each one they examined but were quite open to being bribed into saying they'd found nothing wrong . . .

Why the deceit? Basically, once a household had been visited and a member found to have died from the disease, the house was sealed up for 40 days and a red cross painted on the door. Special guards with nasty looking halberds (big choppers) patrolled the deserted streets to make sure no one broke out. Just imagine it. After 40 days all the inhabitants were usually dead.

Don't Panic!

In order to stop widespread panic, the weekly newsletters gave the causes of death as any of the following:

 dropsy

 griping of the guts

 winde (death by farting – I think not*)

 worms

* I thought we'd agreed on the term 'breaking wind' for that word. Ed

- French pox
- frighted
- plain lethargy

By July, two thousand were dying every week and anyone with any money (or sense) was quitting the city. This wasn't as easy as it sounds, as most of the villages and towns around London were under strict orders to frighten off or even kill anyone trying to get into their as yet plague-free space.

A freezing winter kept the whole sorry business at bay (plagues hate to be chilly) but by April of the following year, it was admitted that loads more had gone and died a horrid death. There was a rush to build new 'pest houses' or hospitals but they became so oversubscribed that eventually visitors had to walk across the beds to see their nearest and dearest. I don't know about you, but I'm not sure I'd be visiting plague victims at all . . .

Time to Go!

The extremely well-to-do rushed off to their country houses (or simply bought them quick), so by the summer of 1658 there wasn't a nobleman, merchant, clergyman, doctor, lawyer or judge to be found in the city for love nor money. Bad news if you were feeling a little under the weather (or wanted to get married) but brilliant if you'd just murdered someone. Nutty prophets toured the streets screaming 'Forty days and London shall be destroyed', which must have cheered the citizens up no end.

Abandoned servants, faced with no jobs, went on the rampage, sometimes robbing their own masters' houses, or forming gangs to loot other deserted homes. Others were put to work leading the horse-drawn carts to the burial grounds, but they usually died or simply deserted, leaving the poor nags to wander the streets, aimlessly trailing their hideous cargo of stiff ex-Londoners.

It was mayhem.

Useless Fact No. 717

Although fortunes were made by quack doctors selling bogus potions and pills, the burning of saltpetre and amber in one's house sometimes had a good effect. Not because it cured the poxy disease, but because it seemed to keep the rats, and their little chums, the fleas, at bay.

Where to Put Them

Very soon all the regular downtown cemeteries were full to bursting, with corpses turning up every day by the cart-load. The whole of London reeked with the stench of rotting bodies. Despite the numerous plague pits that were dug all around, corpses often lay in festering piles by the sides of the road (and we think London's a mess now!).

ROOM FOR TWO MORE INSIDE

Plagues to Go

Plagues (like rats) don't normally confine themselves to cities, and the epidemic soon spread throughout a not very Merrie England. Some smaller villages were wiped out entirely while others guarded their incoming roads to stop anyone bringing the disease from elsewhere. Hundreds of terrified escapees from London literally starved to death as they wandered from village to village, pelted with rotten vegetables* or manure from their somewhat unsympathetic country cousins.

By the time the plague began to subside in 1666, 68,595 out of the 460,000 Londoners were underground (dead). On February 1, King Charles nervously crept back into London and that seemed to be a signal for all the other rich folk to return to their probably looted homes.

Not All Bad

Much later the epidemic was regarded as rather a good thing, especially by the rich and educated. 'The Poor Man's Plague',

* If they were starving, why didn't they eat the veg? *Ed*

as it was sometimes called, helped relieve society of vast numbers of London's starving and unemployed, who were becoming a bit of a nuisance. Every cloud has a silver lining, I suppose.*

Useless Fact No. 719

As well as the relaxation of censorship and tolerance of loose living, the Restoration had promoted loads of fundamental scientific questioning (Newton, the Royal Society, etc.), and many people thought that this was blasphemous (rude to God). The Great Plague, the Great Fire (next) and those darned Dutch in the Medway were seen by some religious types as a punishment from God.

The Great Fire

Whether or not God had anything to do with it, London's luck certainly was somewhere completely else. In the same year as the Plague survivors were burying the last of their dead, a fire broke out in a humble baker's shop in Pudding Lane. The guv'nor and his wife and kids escaped over the roof, but their maid was sadly 'baked' to a crisp. The Lord Mayor, who was called out of bed in the middle of the night, wasn't that impressed at the beginning, exclaiming 'Pish, a woman might p*ss it out!'

Be that as it may, there wasn't a lady of suitable inclination (or bladder capacity) around, and because the streets were so narrow that the occupants could shake hands across the gap, it was a doddle for the hungry flames, caught in a freak summer wind, to leap across street after wooden street. When it finally burned itself out, 463 acres had been razed to the ground, including 87 churches and 13,200 houses.

* Sometimes I can't believe how sympathetic you are. Ed

Useless Fact No. 721

Robert Hubert, a very silly Frenchman, confessed to having set light to the baker's. This was fine, as the powers that be were dying to blame the French or at least a Catholic (best of all, a French Catholic). Poor Monsieur Hubert turned out to be round the bend and, later on, it was proved that the strange young *homme* wasn't even in London when the fire broke out. Not that it did him any good – he was later hanged at Tyburn.

Useless Fact No. 723

The only good thing about the fire was that it burned so deeply into London's very sub-soil, that it killed most of the remaining plague germs. There was never to be another major outbreak again.*

* Yet! *Ed*

Chapter 9

TRAVEL AND TRADE
OR . . .
HOW TO GET NOWHERE
VERY FAST

If you want to go to Birmingham or Brighton, Chiswick or Chester, you can either jump in the car or coach, go to the station or, if you're as fabulously rich as I am, just get out your personal jet or helicopter.* In Stuart times, roads were practically non-existent, and merely travelling a few miles to the launderette could be a nightmare. The main method of getting around was horse, either on its back or in the cart that it dragged behind it. Stuart England (sounds like a footballer) must have appeared a massive place for 99% of the country people, who rarely strayed more than a few miles from where they were born. The rest of the world must have seemed like another universe, especially as information about foreign parts was scant and exaggerated to say the least.

As for travelling at night, forget it! Not only were there no street lights, but the roads became sun-baked assault courses in the summer, and gloopy, bottomless quagmires in the winter. Either way, they could have your horse or coach on its side in a trice. In addition, there were very few signposts, no street names and, even worse, horrid highwaymen and beastly bands

* You're joking. We don't pay you enough for roller-skates. Ed

of really rough ruffians were ever willing to relieve you of your money or your life (or wife).

Even worse . . .

Travel actually became more difficult as the Stuart era ground on. The Enclosure movement was a right pain in the . . . saddle for the regular traveller, for what had once been a straightish trek across open ground was now a lane that forced them to twist and turn in order to avoid crossing and squashing someone's crops. (That's why Roman roads were so straight – they didn't have to worry about such things, and probably wouldn't have anyway.) Also, with the huge increase in carriages, the ruts became far deeper and more numerous and almost impassable.

Useless Fact No. 726

The first toll gates, allowed by an Act of Parliament in 1663, went some way towards improving the roads as they were designed to collect money for repairs.

Post Haste

On all the main roads to and from London, the countless inns kept spare post horses to be used in relay by the Royal Mail service (recently invented by the Tudors). These horses could usually be hired (threepence a mile and sixpence for a guide) and the postmasters made quite a killing on the side for themselves and the inn-keeper, who could charge almost what he liked for the stabling.

Useless Fact No. 729

The postal system as we know and love it today, was set up during the reign of Charles I. Postboys would leave London and drop their bags at individual towns (all letters had to go through the city) and from these towns, bags of mail would be sent to the individual village postmasters. They'd then send other postboys out to the person named on the envelope – all for tuppence a time.

Stagecoach Travel

The first stagecoaches trundled out of London during the Stuart era from a rank in the Strand. Progress was terribly slow (a day to do 50 miles) as everything was pretty much governed by the weather, which in turn governed the state of the roads.

Water Travel

In bygone days, rivers were used far more as a method of

getting around. It was often quicker to row a boat than suffer the terrible roads. In big towns with rivers, watermen were like early taxi drivers, and at one time, especially in London, you could practically cross the Thames, bank to bank, stepping from one taxi-boat (or 'wherry') to another.

The first Hackney carriages half scared these watermen to death, as they saw it as the end of their monopoly. If you look at the deserted Thames these days, you'll see that they had a point.

Useless Fact No. 732

Talking of death, one morning in February 1692, eleven passengers who'd been travelling down the Thames were found, frozen solid by a snap frost that had seized up the river.

Useless Fact No. 737

Owing to the shallowness of the water and the old, wooden London Bridge slowing its flow to a near standstill, the Thames froze solid every year. Massive Frost Fairs were held on the ice, with every kind of entertainment and elaborate temporary stalls from bank to bank.

Abroad – Wherever that Was

Few people in Stuart times ever travelled abroad for pleasure, partly because of the danger of the unknown, partly because of the great expense and partly because one needed a blinking licence to do so. Having said this, hardly any of the coastline was ever watched, so slipping in and out was dead easy if you knew what you were doing.

The first stop-off was usually France, Spain or Holland, and to give you some idea of the cost, the fare from Dover to Calais by packet-boat was £5 (far more, in proportion, than now). But these boats were often crowded and deadly slow. It was quicker to get a few guys to row you across if you were in a hurry.

Grand Tour

Perhaps the other most common bunch of travellers abroad were young noblemen and their tutors (for *tutors* read *servants*) doing rather arty Grand Tours of Europe before settling down to the drudge of marriage (in other words – a last fling). This was always expensive and sometimes dangerous, as those dratted foreigners saw these young rich kids, who often spent most of their time in sleazy bars and cafés, as easy pickings. Many were reported back in England as kidnapped or murdered (or worse!).

Rough Trade

Merchants, on the other hand, were buzzing all over the place with charters from the crown allowing them to trade in foreign parts. These traders had to be pretty good fighters and had to deal with a pretty varied load of not very pretty people. Apart from their normal customers who paid, and those who wanted to flog them other goods, there was another lot who wanted the goods but didn't want to stump up the cash for them (technical term: pirates).

It was the traders themselves who built the forts and supplied many of the soldiers to protect their foreign investments. The British government had made it plain that, athough they were happy to take a cut of the profits, once these brave soldiers of fortune had left our shores they were well and truly on their own. And those profits were seriously huge, which meant that massive outfits, like the all-powerful East India Company, could operate in far distant lands wielding more clout than the very government of the country they came from. Woe betide anyone if they tried to muscle in on any of the areas that they'd put aside for themselves. A lot of the mini-wars and feuds throughout the world, during the Stuart epoch, were therefore not between countries, as you might imagine, but were furious armed squabbles amongst greedy traders, Dutch, Spanish, English, you name it, trying either to protect or to snatch new territories.

Pirates Ahoy!

Our trading ships were armed to the gunwhales (pronounced 'gunnels'). They had to be, as the Royal Navy didn't lift a finger or anything else to protect them. The worst threat of all was from the spine-chilling Turkish pirates who took 466 of our merchant ships between 1609 and 1616 and later, in 1625, took 27 vessels in ten days, carting off a thousand of our poor sailor boys (the ones they didn't hack to pieces) as slaves. Even little old England was surrounded by pirates, bobbing in and out of the countless little creeks in Devon and Cornwall,

pillaging the local villages and scoffing all their cream teas. Shocking! I mean, cream's really bad for you.

Useless Fact No. 739

At one time they even had to blow out the shipping lights on the Lizard Peninsula because they were becoming of far more use to pirate ships than anyone else. There were even a load of sneaky Spanish frigates lurking off Land's End waiting to pick off our merchant ships as they left the West Country.

A Right Rotten Royal Navy

While talking of boats and stuff, a few words should be said about the state of our navy in those days. Ever since the Elizabethan era, the job of sailor in the British fleet was seldom to be recommended. On board these – for want of a better word – ships (often not much more than rotting, leaking hulks)

the poor ragged devils were semi-starved, seldom paid and forced to stay on board for fear of a good whipping or keelhauling (the jolly practice of dragging a sailor right under the keel of the boat by ropes, so that the barnacles could scrape the skin from his body).

Useless Fact No. 742

Many of these disgusting hulks (the ones that hadn't sunk) became the terrifying prison ships and plague hospitals that were all the rage in Stuart times.

HOW DO I GET ROOM SERVICE?

Charles I, though doing precious little for the conditions of his sorry sailors, maintained a force of 41 men-of-war (ships!), but in the two years following his death it was doubled – and for good reason. Everyone at that time hated Cromwell's Puritan England and they all took advantage of the Spanish war to attack us even if they'd got nothing to do with Spain. Served 'em right, I say.

ᓂ– TIME'S UP

I hope you now agree that the Stuart period left rather a lot to be desired, quality-of-life-wise. Anyway, I've finished this mighty work (no more words left) and it's time to move on to something else (the dole queue, probably).

If you enjoyed it and would like to find out more, might I suggest you get thyself down to thy school or local library and dive into more specific subjects, like the plague or the Great Fire – you won't be disappointed.

If you don't want to be bothered with loads of pages and just want to get to the point fast, might I humbly suggest that you buy another of the books in this series. They may not be great literature, but they're short and – more to the point – dead cheap.